The Quotation Bank for A-Level

Death Of A Salesman

Arthur Miller

Copyright © 2023 Esse Publishing Limited and Carl Cerny
The moral rights of the authors have been asserted.

First published in 2023 by:
The Quotation Bank
Esse Publishing Limited
10 9 8 7 6 5 4 3 2 1

All rights reserved. No part of this publication may be reproduced, resold, stored in a retrieval system or transmitted in any form, or by any means (electronic, photocopying, mechanical or otherwise) without the prior written permission of both the copyright owners and the publisher.

A CIP catalogue record for this book is available from the British Library.
ISBN 978-1-7396080-3-3

All enquiries to: contact@thequotationbank.co.uk
Every effort has been made to trace and contact all relevant copyright holders. However, if contacted the publisher will rectify any omission or error at the earliest opportunity.

Printed and bound by Target Print Limited, Broad Lane, Cottenham, Cambridge CB24 8SW.

www.thequotationbank.co.uk

Introduction

How The Quotation Bank can help you in your exams   4
How to use The Quotation Bank   5

Quotations

Act One   6
Act Two   16
Requiem   29
Critical and Contextual Quotations   31

Revision and Essay Planning

Performance History   41
How to revise effectively   42
Suggested revision activities   43
Glossary   44

Welcome to The Quotation Bank, the comprehensive guide to all the key quotations you need to succeed in your exams.

Whilst you may have read the play, watched a film adaptation, understood the plot and have a strong grasp of context, all questions in your A-Levels require you to write a focused essay, full of textual references and quotations (be they textual, critical or contextual), and most importantly, quotations that you then analyse.

I think we all agree it is **analysis** that is the tricky part – and that is why we are here to help!

The Quotation Bank takes 25 of the most important quotations from the text, interprets them, analyses them, highlights literary and dramatic techniques Miller has used, puts them in context, and suggests which quotations you might use in which essays. We have also included 10 contextual and critical quotations, analysed them, and linked them closely to the text, all for you to explore.

At the end of **The Quotation Bank** we have put together a performance history and great revision exercises to help you prepare for your exam. We have also included a detailed glossary to make sure you completely understand what certain literary terms actually mean!

How The Quotation Bank can help you in your exams.

The Quotation Bank is designed to make sure every point you make in an essay clearly fulfils the Assessment Objectives an examiner will be using when marking your work.

Every quotation comes with the following detailed material:

Interpretation: The interpretation of each quotation allows you to fulfil **AO1**, articulating an informed, personal response, and **AO5**, using different interpretations to inform your exploration of the text.

Techniques: Using associated concepts and terminology (in this case, the techniques used by Miller) is a key part of **AO1**, and can help you identify and analyse ways in which meanings are shaped (**AO2**).

Analysis: We have provided as much analysis (**AO2**) as possible, as well as exploring the significance and influence of contextual material (**AO3**) and different interpretations (**AO5**). It is a great idea to analyse the quotation in detail – you need to do more than just say what it means, but also try to explore a variety of different ways of interpreting it.

Use in essays on… Your answer needs to be focused to fulfil **AO1**. This section helps you choose relevant quotations and link them together for a stronger, more detailed essay.

How to use The Quotation Bank.

Many students spend time learning quotations by heart. This can be useful, but it is important to remember what you are meant to do with quotations once you get into the exam.

By using **The Quotation Bank**, not only will you have a huge number of textual, critical and contextual quotations to use in your essays, you will also have ideas on what to say about them, how to analyse them, how to link them together, and what questions to use them for.

These quotations can form the basis of your answer, making sure every point **articulates an informed, personal response (AO1)** and allows you to **analyse ways in which meanings are shaped (AO2)**.

The critical and contextual quotations allow you to easily and effectively explore the significance and influence of **context (AO3)**, and provide you with a variety of **different readings to explore (AO5).**

The textual quotations cover the whole text to allow you to show comprehensive whole text knowledge, and the critical and contextual quotations cover the full range of the text's publication history to help you explore the contexts in which the text was both **written and received (AO3)**.

Act One:

> **STAGE DIRECTIONS:** *"We are aware of towering, angular shapes behind [the house], surrounding it on all sides. […] As more light appears, we see a solid vault of apartment houses around the small, fragile-seeming home. An air of the dream clings to the place, a dream rising out of reality."*

Interpretation: This powerful opening stage direction, sometimes described as a prose poem, establishes the urban and domestic setting of the play while hinting at the vulnerable, "fragile-seeming" state of the Loman family as symbolised through their home.

Techniques: Symbolism; Foreshadowing; Staging.

Analysis:

- The densely populated urban setting, "surrounding it on all sides", invites the audience to see the struggles of the Loman family as just one example of the many families living in similar conditions with the same challenges and frustrations.
- The oppressive presence of tower blocks loom over the Loman home, stifling their upward social aspirations. Closed in "on all sides", there is a sense of imprisonment, unable to see beyond their immediate surroundings. "Vault" evokes conflicting associations of deathly tombs, or of locked cabinets protecting items of value.
- "The dream" alludes to The American Dream; it seems insubstantial, ephemeral, "fragile" and constantly "rising" out of reach while it also "clings to" or suffocates the home.

Use in essays on… The American Dream; Hope; Natural vs Human World; Family.

Act One:
> **WILLY: "It's all right. I came back." LINDA: "Why? What happened? (*Slight pause.*) Did something happen, Willy?"**

Interpretation: Returning tired from a day's work, the play's opening dialogue between Willy Loman and his worried wife Linda immediately establishes a tone of concern and anxiety.

Techniques: Foreshadowing; Repetition.

Analysis:
- Willy's reassurance to Linda ("I came back") implies there might be some reason why she would not have expected him to return. The audience gets an early impression Willy may spend nights away from the family home, hinting at an untrustworthy character and foreshadowing later revelations about his infidelities.
- The hurried repetition of questions conveys a sense of panic from Linda: she clearly worries about him. "Why? What happened?" suggests she was not expecting him to come "back". The relationship is introduced as one typical of the period: the man away from home to work whilst the woman waits in the domestic setting for his return.
- Willy, a diminutive form of the more commanding William, infantilises him. A character known as 'Willy' (with its inevitable juvenile and phallic associations) is perhaps unlikely to become one of the great heroes of modern drama. The passage that follows, describing his confusion while driving, seems to confirm this.

Use in essays on… Relationships; Betrayal; Family.

Act One:
> **WILLY:** "Biff Loman is lost. In the greatest country in the world a young man with such – personal attractiveness, gets lost. And such a hard worker. There's one thing about Biff – he's not lazy."

Interpretation: Willy expresses disappointment at Biff's inability to live up to his ambitions for his adult life, introducing the problematic father-son relationship at the core of the play.

Techniques: Irony; Tone.

Analysis:

- Willy seems to agree with Linda's previous statement ("I think he's very lost") whilst contradicting what he said moments earlier ("Biff is a lazy bum!"). The rapid change in tone suggests Willy is easily confused, erratic in his outlook, and that he has a troubling mixture of conflicting feelings towards his son: pride and disappointment.
- Willy speaks with a strong national pride, declaring America, "the greatest country in the world". There is a sad irony here; it is the capitalism upon which modern America was built that has driven Willy to become a dissatisfied and pathetic figure, full of misguided ambition and misplaced confidence.
- The attributes held by Willy as most valuable are "personal attractiveness" and being a "hard worker". This hints at the fragility of superficial appearances, and begins to reveal Miller's critique of a culture predicated upon individualism and industry.

Use in essays on… The American Dream; Family; Delusion; Masculinity; Identity.

Act One:
> **WILLY:** "There's more people! That's what's ruining this country! Population is getting out of control. The competition is maddening! Smell the stink from that apartment house! And another one of the other side…"

Interpretation: Willy bemoans societal changes and his frustrations with the urban life in New York, with undertones of xenophobic hostility to the influx of migrants evident in his panic about the pace of social change.

Techniques: Tone; Irony.

Analysis:
- Shortly before this line, Willy expresses frustration at the damage done to the natural world by the rapid development of an urbanising landscape ("The grass don't grow any more, you can't raise a carrot in the back yard.") He mourns the loss of an idyllic and bucolic past while, ironically, not recognising he is of course part of the alleged problem.
- If we assume the Lomans are migrants to New York, as many such families were at the time, then Willy's lines assume an even deeper tone of irony. With this perspective, his family contributes to the "out of control" population and "maddening" competition.
- This line cuts directly over Linda's more tentative comments; Willy is an assertive, argumentative man who speaks with a degree of assumed authority on the city's social dynamics. The pessimistic "ruining" juxtaposes earlier comments on America's greatness.

Use in essays on… The American Dream; The Past; Natural vs Human World.

Act One:

> **WILLY:** "Biff, up in Albany I saw a beautiful hammock. I think I'll buy it next trip, and we'll hang it right between those two elms. Wouldn't that be something?"

Interpretation: The first of many flashbacks to moments in the family's past, this image of closeness between Willy and Biff contrasts their unsettled relationship in the present.

Techniques: Symbolism; Irony; Flashback.

Analysis:

- The symbol of the hammock is a potent one, representing the future comfort Willy aspires to achieve. Sadly, not only does Willy inform us earlier that the elm trees get cut down, but even in his senior years he is still compelled to continue working, driven by his desire to earn money and build his reputation. The comfort he dreams of never comes, and Miller develops his critique of American attitudes towards a Sisyphean life of work.
- The flashback technique is frequently used as a key feature of Miller's 'subjective realism' dramatic style. The fluidity with which the past intrudes on the present in Willy's mind builds the impression of a character in a fragile mental state, unable to adapt to changing times, constantly seeking comfort by reliving moments in life he can remember fondly.
- The significant reference to "buy[ing]" the hammock indicates the importance of monetary power and material consumption to a capitalist outlook.

Use in essays on… The American Dream; The Past; Hope; Delusion.

Act One:

WILLY: "The man who makes an appearance in the business world, the man who creates personal interest, is the man who gets ahead. Be liked and you will never want."

Interpretation: Willy criticises the bookish boyhood neighbour Bernard and celebrates what he values in his sons: popularity and physical strength. Miller highlights the misguided advice Willy offers to younger men to highlight his delusions about his place in the world.

Techniques: Irony; Repetition.

Analysis:

- The repeated use of the noun "man" makes clear Willy is speaking about the role of men at the exclusion of women, reflecting his patriarchal outlook. "Gets ahead" points to the competitive foundations of capitalist society, while "appearance" illustrates once more the fragile nature of surface appearances which are so fundamental to Willy's world view.
- The closing phrase, "Be liked and you will never want" seems to serve as Willy's personal motto or maxim: the desire for popularity and approval drive many of his actions and after this line he boastfully proclaims, "I never have to wait in line to see a buyer".
- Although the speech is given to both Biff and his younger brother Happy, it is implied Willy is offering this advice to Biff in particular. After this speech, Biff asks a question to which Willy replies; when Happy contributes with his own question, he is ignored.

Use in essays on… Masculinity; Delusion; Identity; Legacy.

Act One:

WILLY: "Did you see the ceiling I put up in the living room?"

Interpretation: Speaking to Charley, Willy seeks approval for his manual skills in making domestic improvements to his house. It is one of many instances when Miller stresses Willy's pleasure and skill in manual work, suggesting this may have been a more fitting path for him.

Techniques: Symbolism; Irony.

Analysis:

- There are frequent symbols of entrapment, imprisonment, suffocation, and restriction; the "ceiling" Willy boasts of erecting is one such symbol. In this case, however, rather than being imposed upon him and the family (such as the towering apartment blocks described in the opening stage directions), this one has been put in place by Willy himself.
- Despite lofty ambitions for his family (and Biff in particular), he ironically limits their development through his out-dated and delusional attitudes towards work, masculinity, and success. Later, Willy instructs Biff to paint the ceiling and, in a gesture which illuminates his resistance to his father's ideals, Biff refuses.
- Boastful of his achievements and refusing to give Charley advice on how to put up a ceiling himself, Willy later declares, "A man who can't handle tools is not a man. You're disgusting." The cruelty with which Willy attacks Charley seems vicious, hinting at jealousy held by Willy given the success of Charley's son, the successful lawyer Bernard.

Use in essays on… Masculinity; Delusion; Family; Identity.

Act One:
BEN: "Father was a very great and a very wild-hearted man. […] he'd toss the whole family into the wagon, and then he'd drive the team right across the country […] and sell the flutes that he'd made on the way."

Interpretation: A vision of Willy's brother, Ben, intrudes upon his dialogue with Charley; they relive memories of childhood and discuss decisions they have taken throughout their younger adult years. This establishes Willy's confused state and his idolisation of his brother.

Techniques: Flashback; Juxtaposition; Symbolism.

Analysis:
- Although brothers, Ben is a father figure to Willy and his exotic travels and financial success juxtapose Willy's mundane and modest lifestyle: compare Ben's travels to African diamond mines with Willy's sales trips to Yonkers. Ben celebrates his father's pioneering spirit ("wild-hearted" and "drive the team"), praising the spirit of adventure and courage that characterised many Americans seeking their fortune in the mid-nineteenth century.
- "The flutes that he'd [their father] made" illustrate the resourceful self-sufficiency crucial to success in business, and serve an important symbolic function. The flute melody heard throughout the play – sometimes referred to as Willy's Theme – serves as a subtle reminder of this adventurous and pioneering past in the Loman family, perhaps taunting Willy with his failure to achieve the greatness accomplished by his brother.

Use in essays on… The Past; The American Dream; Family; Legacy.

Act One:
   LINDA: "I don't say he's a great man. […] But he's a human being, and a terrible thing is happening to him. So attention must be paid. […] Attention, attention must be finally paid to such a person."

Interpretation: Linda's insistence that "such a person" deserves the respect of his sons, despite his modest accomplishments, presents her loyalty to Willy in spite of himself.

Techniques: Repetition; Dramatic Irony; Imperative.

Analysis:
- Although Miller took issue with this simplistic interpretation, critics explored whether "Loman" reflects Willy's status as a 'low man': a "human being" of limited potential and modest achievement, representing the 'everyman' of society. Through Linda, Miller, who identified strongly with the ordinary working man, foregrounds Willy's humanity, challenging attitudes whereby a man's respectability is based on his wealth or fame.
- Repetition of "attention" literally calls an audience's attention to this essential point in the play: a wife demanding ("must") her son respect his father despite his shortcomings.
- Earlier we observe a flashback to Willy's relationship with The Woman. Aware of his past infidelities, we pity Linda's total devotion to a deeply flawed husband. Later we find Biff witnessed Willy's affair, understanding more fully his dismissal of Willy in lines such as, "He always, always wiped the floor with you. Never had an ounce of respect for you."

Use in essays on… Relationships; Betrayal; Family; The Past.

Act One:
HAPPY: "I'm gonna get married, Mom. I wanted to tell you." LINDA: "Go to sleep, dear."

Interpretation: Happy, desperate for attention and approval from his parents, is ignored by Linda when he shares exciting news. Often regarded as Willy's replacement at the end of the play, his struggle to get noticed echoes his father's obsessive, unsuccessful quest for approval.

Techniques: Repetition; Tone.

Analysis:

- Happy frequently repeats "I lost weight, Pop", often at times when Willy's focus is on Biff, whether encouraging, chastising, or instructing him. The repetition indicates a desire to please his father who is so concerned by appearances, yet he is repeatedly ignored.
- Here there is an even more desperate attempt to gain attention as he breaks the news to his mother. She also ignores him with the infantilising, dismissive, "go to sleep, dear" before Willy returns the focus to reliving Biff's celebrated Ebbets Field football game.
- In some ways, Happy epitomises twentieth century American values. His name recalls the founding principles of the United States ("Life, liberty, and the pursuit of <u>happiness</u>" in the *Declaration of Independence*) and he aspires to common goals of working American (and heterosexual) men: "My own apartment, a car, and plenty of women". But he, like Biff, is jaded and disenchanted, and there is an ironic edge to Miller's naming of his character.

Use in essays on… Relationships; Hope; Family; Identity.

Act Two:
> **LINDA: "Not enough sun gets back there. Nothing'll grow any more."**

Interpretation: Linda responds to Willy's comment, "I'd like to buy some seeds", with this bleak image of a barren garden, cast over by the shadow of the high-rise buildings encircling their garden.

Techniques: Imagery; Symbolism.

Analysis:

- Linda's comment is a powerful symbol for the failures and disappointments of the Loman family. Through her line Miller subtly draws our attention to their declining fortunes by contrasting the brightness ("sun") of the past (it is implied that things used to "grow" in the garden), the gloomy barrenness of the present (with the garden cast over by the shadow of the surrounding buildings), and the hopelessness of the future.
- The line also illustrates the changes which have occurred around the Loman family: the high-rise buildings around the garden have been recently built and stifle the sense of opportunity ("nothing'll grow") available to the family.
- It is not often in the play that we see Linda directly challenge or contradict Willy and these words are surrounded by phrases which placate him by entertaining his ideas ("That'd be wonderful" and "You'll do it yet dear"). In not wanting to spoil Willy's dreams, Linda is complicit in his delusion and permits his indulgence in these fantasies.

Use in essays on… Hope; Delusion; The Past; Relationships; Natural vs Human World.

Act Two:
WILLY: "What could be more satisfying than to be able to go, at the age of eighty-four, into twenty or thirty different cities, and pick up a phone, and be remembered and loved and helped by so many different people? […] he died the death of a salesman."

Interpretation: Willy explains his entry into the sales profession. Faced with the choice to either follow the "streak of self-reliance" of his father and brother to Alaska, or pursue the kind of popularity achieved by Dave Singleman, Willy opted for the latter.

Techniques: Irony; Tri-colon.

Analysis:
- Willy venerates the accomplishments of the successful Dave Singleman, whose death is described with the phrase Miller eventually chose for the play's title (after abandoning the original title, '*The Inside of His Head*').
- At the age of "eighteen, nineteen", Willy was impressed by Singleman's popularity. Although his age is revealed ("eighty-four"), Willy either ignored or underestimated the lifetime of work required to build such a reputation – there is no recognition from Willy that to be still visiting "twenty or thirty different cities" at that age is not what many would wish for (perhaps not even Singleman himself).
- The contrast between Willy and Singleman is stark; in the twilight of his career Willy enjoys none of the popularity ("remembered and loved and helped") he aimed to achieve.

Use in essays on… Delusion; The American Dream; Legacy; Identity.

Act Two:
BEN: "You've a new continent on your doorstep, William. Get out of these cities, they're full of talk and time payments and courts of law. Screw on your fists and you can fight for a fortune up there."

Interpretation: This moment of analepsis enters Willy's thoughts straight after his failed meeting with Howard. Reliving a moment when he had an opportunity to take a different, perhaps more lucrative path with Ben in Alaska, he is taunted by the road not taken.

Techniques: Flashback; Juxtaposition.

Analysis:
- Ben speaks of the pioneering spirit of those who settled (or, as some would argue, colonised) America in the mid-nineteenth century when it was still perceived as a "new continent" full of boundless opportunity for those with the adventurous spirit and rugged individualism required to thrive in such conditions.
- Ben speaks to Willy with a respectful appellation no other character uses, addressing him with the more formal, perhaps ennobling, "William" rather than "Willy".
- Ben juxtaposes the banalities and bureaucracy of "talk and time payments and courts of law" with the thrill of a life in the wilds of Alaska. A lifestyle suited to strong, confident, self-reliant men ("fists" "fight" and "fortune"), perhaps it would never have suited the "foolish" Willy in any case: he was doomed to mediocrity.

Use in essays on… The American Dream; Masculinity; Natural vs Human World; The Past.

Act Two:
WILLY: "I'm – I'm overjoyed to see how you made the grade, Bernard, overjoyed. It's an encouraging thing to see a young man really – really…Looks very good for Biff – very…(*He breaks off, then*) Bernard… (*He is so full of emotion, he breaks off again.*) […] How - how did you? Why didn't he ever catch on?"

Interpretation: Willy struggles to compliment Bernard's success before his jealousy becomes clear, highlighting his disappointment in the accomplishments of his sons - in particular Biff.

Techniques: Language; Sentence Structure.

Analysis:

- Willy's stuttered, repetitive phrasing hints at a lack of sincerity, struggling to find words to articulate mixed feelings about Bernard's successes as a "young man".
- The sudden interruption to his compliments signals a shift to what Willy wants to know from Bernard: why he has become so much more successful than Biff. "So full of emotion" indicates this is really what he cares about, rather than simply congratulating Bernard and taking altruistic pleasure in his accomplishments.
- Significantly, Willy's questions focus on what Bernard did, and what Biff did not do, to secure a successful and promising future. Willy does not ask what he could have done differently as a father, perhaps highlighting his lack of responsibility for – or awareness of – his influence on his son's path.

Use in essays on…Relationships; The Past; Family; Legacy; Masculinity.

Act Two:
> BIFF: "Who was it, Pop? Who ever said I was a salesman with Oliver?" WILLY: "Well, you were." BIFF: "No, Dad, I was a shipping clerk." WILLY: "But you were practically –" BIFF: (*with determination*) "Dad, I don't know who said it first, but I was never a salesman for Bill Oliver."

Interpretation: This dialogue exposes Biff's frustration at his father's delusions. Much more honest and accountable than his father, Biff challenges the falsehoods and fantasies Willy constructs and in doing so, Miller presents a troubled and fractious relationship.

Techniques: Language; Tone; Sentence Structure.

Analysis:
- The increasingly forceful tone in which Biff has to challenge Willy's delusional untruths show the audience Biff's exasperation with his father. While Biff's words intensify, Willy's assertions weaken, descending from "you were" to "you were practically", demonstrating the fundamental differences between the two men.
- The lie Willy told about Biff was that he had been a salesman like his father, underscoring his desperation to be perceived as a man of influence: one who might have inspired his son to follow in his career path rather than be nothing more than a "shipping clerk". Sadly, Willy has no such inspiring influence on the adult Biff, who is acutely aware of his father's flaws.

Use in essays on…Delusion; The Past; Family; Relationships; Identity.

Act Two:

> **WILLY:** "I'm not interested in stories about the past or any crap of that kind because the woods are burning boys, you understand? There's a big blaze going on all around. I was fired today."

Interpretation: In an agitated tone, Willy distances himself from fantasies of the past as Biff instructs "Let's hold onto the facts tonight, Pop". In a powerful moment of pathos, Willy confesses "I was fired", juxtaposing the celebratory intent of the restaurant visit.

Techniques: Imagery; Foreshadowing; Metaphor; Sentence Structure.

Analysis:

- The pastoral metaphor "the woods are burning" is unusual for Willy, a man closely linked with the city; it seems more appropriate for Ben, who made his fortune in the forests of Alaska. Perhaps memories of Ben are impacting on Willy, shown through the metaphor.
- The blunt and abrupt phrasing of "I was fired today" is contrasted with the much more dramatic phrase, "There's a big blaze going on all around". The metaphor of fire combined with the hellish – perhaps apocalyptic – imagery may foreshadow the downfall of the play's hero as his life unravels following the loss of his character-defining job.
- Shortly after, the powerful impact of this news on Willy's sons softens their attitude towards him, with Happy accepting some of Willy's delusions ("Sure he went up there") while Biff struggles to stick firmly to facts ("Yeah, he gave me a couple of – no, no!").

Use in essays on… Delusion; Betrayal; The Past; Natural vs Human World; Identity.

Act Two:
> BIFF: "Dad…" WILLY: "She's nothing to me, Biff. I was lonely, I was terribly lonely." BIFF: "You - you gave her Mama's stockings!" (*His tears break through and he rises to go.*)

Interpretation: Occurring towards the end of the flashback in The Standish Arms exposing Willy's infidelities, further light is cast on the causes of Biff and Willy's troubled relationship.

Techniques: Foreshadowing; Irony.

Analysis:
- Having come to visit his father to confess that he "flunked math", Biff witnesses the intimate affair Willy pursues with the anonymous character 'The Woman'. This irreparably damages Biff's trust in his father; until this point he had idolised him, seen in flashback scenes showing Biff and Happy's boyish excitement to spend time with Willy.
- From the outset of the play the phallic associations with Willy's name have perhaps foreshadowed his sexual indiscretions; Biff's disgust at Willy giving away "Mama's stockings" highlights the intense sense of betrayal in this moment ("his tears break through"), especially given that we frequently see Linda mending her stockings.
- Having been so keen to model attributes of a successful, self-reliant American man to his sons, it is a cruel irony that perhaps the most obvious way Happy and Biff take after their father is in their casual, disrespectful attitude towards sexual relationships with women.

Use in essays on…Betrayal; Relationships; Masculinity; Family; The Past.

Act Two:
WILLY: (*anxiously*) **"Oh, I'd better hurry. I've got to get some seeds. (*He starts off to the right*) I've got to get some seeds, right away. Nothing's planted. I don't have a thing in the ground."**

Interpretation: Having been abandoned by his sons (Biff in a fit of distress, Happy to pursue two female interests), Willy's statement to the waiter powerfully symbolises his desire to make a mark on the world and to leave a legacy for which he will be remembered.

Techniques: Symbolism; Sentence Structure; Repetition.

Analysis:
- The short sentence structures and repetitive phrasing hint at Willy's disorientation and confusion, having just been distracted by a distressing memory, and realising he has been abandoned by his sons.
- Despite his desire to plant "some seeds, right away", the cruel reality – as the audience already knows – is that nothing will grow in their garden any more. The barrenness of their garden ("nothing's planted") combined with Willy's anxious urges to nurture a plant to health highlights the pathos of his situation at this late stage in the play.
- Numerous references to Willy's horticultural interests are subtle reminders of the rustic, rural life he may have preferred with Ben. The musical accompaniment ('Willy's Theme' and the associations with his father's hand-crafted flutes) strengthens this interpretation.

Use in essays on…Delusion; Betrayal; Legacy; Natural vs Human World.

Act Two:

WILLY: "But the funeral – (*straightening up*) Ben, that funeral will be massive! They'll come from Maine, Massachusetts, Vermont, New Hampshire! All the old-timers with the strange license plates – that boy will be thunder-struck, Ben, because he never realized – I am known!"

Interpretation: In another moment of distracted reverie, Willy speaks to Ben who – though present on stage and in Willy's mind – is absent from reality. The hubris with which Willy speaks about his "massive" future funeral intensifies the pitiful state of his burial ceremony when the audience sees the paucity of mourners in the Requiem; there are no "old-timers".

Techniques: Foreshadowing; Sentence Structure; Staging.

Analysis:

- The disconnected syntax develops the presentation of Willy as confused and distressed. During this dialogue with Ben, Willy continues to meticulously plant seeds in carefully measured rows, underscoring his obsession with posthumous legacy.
- Throughout this passage it becomes clear Willy is planning his suicide, referencing a "guaranteed, gilt-edged" plan to make "twenty thousand dollars" for his family through his life insurance policy despite Ben's warnings it is "cowardly". In this way Miller displays Willy's obsessive preoccupation with monetary wealth, providing for his family, and being "known" favourably after his death – all to be achieved at any cost to Willy.

Use in essays on… Legacy; Delusion; Relationships; The American Dream; Family.

Act Two:
BIFF: "I stole myself out of every good job since high school!" WILLY: "And whose fault is that?" BIFF: "And I never got anywhere because you blew me so full of hot air I could never stand taking orders from anybody! That's whose fault it is!"

Interpretation: Escalating towards the climactic moment in their relationship, Biff delivers a series of uncomfortable truths. Blaming Willy for his failures, Biff simultaneously distances himself from Willy while also showing the same trait of evading responsibility for his actions; while originally admitting, "I stole myself out", he ends by placing the "fault" on Willy.

Techniques: Symbolism; Language.

Analysis:
- The frustration Biff shows at Willy's delusional ideas is powerfully expressed through a series of revelations: Happy is not as senior as he has pretended to be; Biff spent time in jail for stealing a suit; and Biff holds Willy responsible ("That's whose fault it is!")
- The significance of Biff's confessions to theft should not be overlooked: it speaks to the materialistic conventions of mid-century America in which perhaps Biff felt compelled to own the trappings of successful professional life despite not having the means to do so.
- Similarly, Biff resents the strong sense of individualism ("never stand taking orders") and self-assurance ("you blew me so full of hot air") instilled in him by Willy. Through Biff, Miller critiques many of the foundational principles underpinning American capitalism.

Use in essays on…Relationships; Masculinity; The Past.

Act Two:
BIFF: "Why am I trying to become what I don't want to be? What am I doing in an office, making a contemptuous, begging fool of myself, when all I want is out there, waiting for me the minute I say I know who I am!"

Interpretation: In this passionate passage Biff challenges the set of values upon which Willy's aspirations are built. Coming towards the end of the play, Miller aims to conclusively dismantle the common perception that a life well-lived is spent working.

Techniques: Repetition; Language.

Analysis:
- Biff's impassioned questions shift from directly challenging Willy to pay attention ("you hear me?") to a more rhetorical style of question ("Why am I trying…What am I doing?") in which Biff challenges the fundamental aspects of Willy's world view.
- Coming towards the end of his story about stealing Bill Oliver's pen (told for the second time in the play), this is a moment of realisation for Biff: he would rather be "out there" with space and time for leisure. The thought is one that has teased Biff during the play but which he never acted upon; "waiting" and "minute" implies it is tantalisingly close.
- In response to this speech, it is significant that Willy "pulls away" rather than directly face his son. Perhaps this indicates the uncomfortable recognition that Biff is making a change Willy never had the courage to make – he remained a "contemptuous, begging fool".

Use in essays on… Masculinity; Delusion; Hope; Family; Natural vs Human World.

Act Two:

BEN: (*with promise*) "It's dark there, but full of diamonds."

Interpretation: As the play reaches the end of Act Two and Willy ushers Linda up to bed, Ben's voice intrudes uncontrollably upon his thoughts. His tantalising and teasing lines draw Willy closer to the suicide he has been considering, showing the power of wealth over the psyche of the common American everyman.

Techniques: Metaphor; Foreshadowing; Repetition.

Analysis:

- The darkness to which Ben refers operates with a double meaning here: on one hand he might be referring to the jungles of Africa where he made his fortune in diamonds, yet on the other hand, "it's dark there" is clearly a metaphor for the death which is imminent for Willy.
- This phrase is repeated in various forms on numerous occasions by Ben, and given the powerful influence Ben has upon Willy's thoughts, it has a persuasive effect on Willy.
- The "promise" in his voice and the optimistic tone of "full", along with Ben's line, "A perfect proposition all round", suggests a degree of certainty that Willy's plan will work; his family will succeed in finally being "full of diamonds".

Use in essays on… The American Dream; Delusion; Hope.

Act Two:
WILLY: (*uttering a gasp of fear, whirling about as if to quiet her*) "Sh!" (*He turns around as if to find his way; sounds, faces, voices, seem to be swarming in upon him and he flicks at them, crying*) "Sh! Sh!" (*Suddenly music, faint and high, stops him. It rises in intensity, almost to an unbearable scream…*) "Shhh!" […] (*There is the sound of a car starting and moving away at full speed. […] As the car speeds off, the music crashes down in a frenzy of sound, which becomes the soft pulsation of a single cello string.*)

Interpretation: The climax of Miller's tragedy depicts a confused, desperate and pitiful man. Realising he is alone on stage, abandoned by his sons, his wife calling to him from offstage, and visions of Ben having vanished, this is a powerfully moving moment in performance.

Techniques: Structure; Symbolism; Staging.

Analysis:

- Willy's inability to speak in this moment – merely shushing voices in his head and crying in "fear" – heightens the sense of pathos. His family are all visible to the audience, within earshot of any calls for help should Willy make them, intensifying his sense of loneliness.
- Sound is important in this dramatic moment; the familiarity of the gentle flute heard during the play is replaced by dissonant, chaotic sounds reflective of Willy's mental state.
- Miller's choice of a car as the mode of death is another example of his outright critique of twentieth-century American consumer capitalism, powerfully symbolised by the motorcar, upon which Willy was so reliant throughout his career as a travelling salesman.

Use in essays on… The American Dream; Betrayal; Family; Legacy.

Requiem:
> **CHARLEY:** "No man only needs a little salary. […] He was a happy man with a batch of cement." […] **BIFF:** "He never knew who he was."

Interpretation: With a small gathering around Willy's graveside, Miller leaves his audience with a sombre tableau to close the play. The bleak scene exposes Willy's delusions about his popularity, with Linda commenting, "Why didn't anybody come?"

Techniques: Structure; Staging.

Analysis:
- In these closing moments of the play – which Miller calls the 'Requiem' – the mourning characters reflect fondly on Willy's life. They make observations on the contradictions in his life, including Biff's remark that "there's more of him in that front stoop than in all the sales he ever made", highlighting the pleasure he took in manual work.
- Charley's short line, "No man only needs a little salary" is heavy with significance here, seeming to be a mouthpiece for Miller himself, whose anti-capitalist stance is clear throughout the play and in others of his oeuvre.
- Following shortly after Biff's realisation that he must first recognise and accept who he is in order to be happy and successful, he notes the comparable struggles faced by Willy who suffered because he, "never knew who he was". It is a painful truth that Willy could never accept he was "happy" with a seemingly mundane "batch of cement."

Use in essays on… Relationships; The American Dream; Masculinity; Identity.

Requiem:
  LINDA: "I made the last payment on the house today. Today, dear. And there'll be nobody home. (*A sob rises in her throat*) We're free and clear. (*Sobbing more fully, released*) We're free. (*Biff comes slowly toward her*) We're free… We're free…"

Interpretation: In these final lines, the audience discovers a bitter, ironic truth; the day of Willy's death was the day of their financial independence, free from mortgage debt. The image of a sobbing widow is a powerful reminder of the damage caused by Willy's delusions.

Techniques: Irony; Tone; Repetition.

Analysis:

- The grim irony of Willy's death coinciding with the last mortgage payment is mirrored by the irony of Linda's repeated utterance, "We're free." The phrase strikes an oddly relieved tone after such a moving scene; Linda is perhaps referring not only to the family's freedom from debt, but also freedom from suffering caused by Willy's misguided dreams.
- Biff's loyalty and care for his mother is shown in his approach and his lifting her to her feet. Having now been cut off from his father's influence, the audience sees him more caring and sensitive than we have until this point. Happy, meanwhile, will continue to pursue his father's dream, to "beat this racket" and "come out number-one man."
- Linda's moving line "there'll be nobody home" implies loneliness. Always overshadowed by her husband and sons in a world dictated by men, her bereavement may represent a kind of emancipation for her; indeed, "I [Linda] made the last payment", not Willy.

Use in essays on… Relationships; Hope; Legacy; Family.

The play's director on its Broadway debut, Elia Kazan (1949), suggested Willy's, "fatal error … is that he built his life and his sense of worth on something completely false: the Opinion of Others. This is the error of our whole capitalist system."

Interpretation: Elia Kazan who, like Arthur Miller, was investigated by the House Committee on Un-American Activities, was a prominent figure in the arts in the mid-twentieth century. Here, he declaims authoritatively on what he perceives to be a social problem in America which he then identifies as Willy's hamartia (fatal flaw). Kazan's use of "fatal" does, however, imply he sees Willy as worthy of being a tragic hero.

Analysis:
- Throughout the play Willy is certainly preoccupied with the "opinion of others"; he seeks attention and approval from many of those characters around him – Charley, The Woman, and Howard, for example.
- While he certainly makes mistakes throughout the play, part of the pity an audience feels for Willy comes, of course, from many things beyond his control. He is partly unable to secure the good opinion of others due to his name, his "foolish" appearance, and his age, each of which undermine his credibility as a man to be taken seriously in business.
- Critical opinions on Willy's character flaws abound but Miller undoubtedly had his own view on the shortcomings of his character: it is believed that Willy was modelled closely on Miller's uncle, Manny.

Use in essays on… Delusion; Identity; Masculinity.

In a *New York Times* essay titled '*Tragedy and the Common Man,*' Miller (1949) states,
"I believe that the common man is as apt a subject for tragedy in its highest sense as kings were … I think the tragic feeling is evoked in us when we are in the presence of a character who is ready to lay down his life, if need be, to secure one thing—his sense of personal dignity."

Interpretation: Critics have discussed extensively whether Willy Loman can be truly considered a tragic hero, and whether *Death of a Salesman* can therefore be considered a genuine tragedy. In this essay Miller defends Loman as a fitting subject for a tragedy and argues for a move away from the traditional Sophoclean tragic form to include "the common man".

Analysis:
- Early modern tragedies (such as Shakespeare's *Hamlet*, Kyd's *The Spanish Tragedy*, and Webster's *The Duchess of Malfi*) and their Greek predecessors (such as Sophocles' *Oedipus Rex*, and Euripedes' *Medea*) set their tragedies amidst "kings" and rulers. Miller challenges this generic convention with a view to paying tribute to the lives of "the common man"; indeed, by viewing them in the "highest sense", he instils a sense of "dignity" in Willy.
- For Miller, the definition of a tragic hero is one who is ready to "lay down his life" to secure "personal dignity". This is, of course, what Willy struggles to achieve; in his final act – suicide – he still does not attain what he has been aiming for throughout the play.

Use in essays on… Hope; Delusion; Identity.

An early commentator on the play and reviewer of the debut production, Brooks Atkinson (1949), remarked,

> "Miller has written a superb drama … It is so simple in style and so inevitable in theme that it scarcely seems like a thing that has been written and acted. For Mr. Miller has looked with compassion into the hearts of some ordinary Americans and quietly transferred their hope and anguish to the theater."

Interpretation: Early reviews of the play were highly favourable, with the debut production scooping major theatrical awards and running for 742 performances. Atkinson finds its strength in the relevance of the story to the ordinary people of America.

Analysis:
- Though he had enjoyed commercial success with *All My Sons* two years earlier, it was *Death of a Salesman* which was hailed as the playwright's masterpiece.
- The play is not, strictly speaking, written in the style of dramatic 'naturalism': with its highly stylised elements, critics have variously described it as "magic realism", "neo-realism" and "mythological realism". However, much of the value found in it by Brooks is a "simple", uncomplicated and honest depiction of the lives of "ordinary Americans".
- Elsewhere in the review, Atkinson states, "What Mr. Miller has achieved somehow seems to belong to everybody." Miller's strong social conscience and interest in the life of the common man (and woman) resonated powerfully with its early audiences.

Use in essays on… Hope; Identity; The American Dream.

Christopher Bigsby (1984) observed,
"In Miller's earliest draft, [Willy says to Biff]: 'To enjoy yourself is not ambition. A tramp has that. Ambition is *things*. A man must want *things, things*. (Miller's emphasis.)"

Interpretation: This line, since edited out of the playscript, provides another moment of Willy instructing Biff on how to live his life as an adult man. The materialistic impulses of the common American man are writ large here, with a father advising his son that the acquisition of "things" is what defines ambition and – with it – success.

Analysis:
- Students of the play may find interest in discussing why Miller removed this line, and whether it would still belong in the play in the final published form.
- The advent of mechanised mass production, commercial advertising, and consumers with plenty of purchasing power in the years immediately after WW2, were the perfect incubator for American consumer capitalism to develop, reflected in Willy's statement.
- Material goods are frequently referenced throughout the play: Willy's Studebaker, Bill Oliver's pen, the stockings, and Ben's diamonds are just a few examples. In each case, however, the material "thing" is tainted with some kind of negative association: the Studebaker is the car Willy drives to his death, the stockings are given to the woman with whom he has an affair, the pen is stolen, and the diamonds are nothing but a fantasy.

Use in essays on… The American Dream; Relationships; Delusion; Hope.

In his autobiography, *Timebends*, Miller (1987) observes that,
   "the idea of creating a new shadow on the earth has never lost its fascination."

Interpretation: Though speaking in general terms, here Miller explains part of the timeless and international relevance of the play's themes, focusing on the human impulse to make a mark and leave a legacy which so obsesses Willy Loman.

Analysis:
- Abandoning the hopes he had for his sons, Willy's attempts to leave a legacy by planting seeds are literally overshadowed by the accomplishments of others. The high-rise buildings that encircle the Loman home cast "a new shadow" over their garden, ensuring nothing Willy plants will ever grow; his hopes for a legacy are stifled and doomed to die.
- Throughout the play, "creating a new shadow" is subtly associated with masculine pride: after all, it is objects which stand phallically erect from the ground which cast a shadow.
- Whilst "on the earth" implies a desire to create something permanent and tangible, the reality is that "idea", "shadow" and "fascination" are abstract and insubstantial.
- The universality of the play's themes have made it highly suitable for adaptation across cultures; indeed, in 1983 Miller himself directed a production for the Beijing People's Art Theatre in communist China.

Use in essays on…Masculinity; Hope; Legacy; Identity.

The playwright David Mamet (1994) argued that,
"The greatest American play, arguably, is the story of a Jew told by a Jew, and cast in "universal" terms. Willy Loman is a Jew in a Jewish industry. But he is never identified as such. His story is never avowed as a Jewish story, and so a great contribution to Jewish, and to Jewish American history is lost. It's lost to the culture as a whole, and, more importantly, it's lost to the Jews, its rightful owners."

Interpretation: Critics have long debated whether the Loman family are Jewish and, if they are, whether it is significant to the play's dramatic effect. Mamet's ire at the play's apparent universality is expressed as the loss of a story he considers to be inherently Jewish in nature.

Analysis:
- The lack of Jewish identity may be painful for Mamet (who is Jewish) given widespread antisemitism which shaped experiences of the Loman family's real-life counterparts.
- More recent critics have continued Mamet's project of reclaiming the Yiddish essence of the play, noting that on the 50th anniversary of the play Miller clarified the Lomans were, "Jews light years away from religion or a community that might have fostered Jewish identity".
- The notion of The American Dream is often criticised for its lack of inclusivity: the right to "life, liberty and the pursuit of happiness" in the Declaration of Independence was not equally accessible to all, excluding minority groups such as Jewish communities.

Use in essays on… The American Dream; Identity.

Interviewed by the BBC to mark his 80th birthday, Miller (1995) remarked,
 [It is about] "what happens when everybody has a refrigerator and a car. I wrote *Salesman* at the beginning of the greatest boom in world history but I felt that the reality was Depression, the whole thing coming down in a heap of ashes. There was still the feel of the Depression, the fear that everything would disappear."

Interpretation: An artist's words on their own work are inevitably illuminating (though not often available). Written in 1949, *Death of a Salesman* is a product of its time, with the post-war economic boom a taunting backdrop for the struggles of Miller's tragic protagonist.

Analysis:
- This comment by the playwright draws attention to the material abundance of the time, with industrial manufacturing processes making high-cost commodities such as refrigerators and cars available to the American middle classes like the Lomans.
- The looming threat of collapse, of "the whole thing coming down", has also been observed in the play text, with some critics noting the frequency of Willy either collapsing or being on the verge of falling.
- "The fear that everything would disappear" is another phrase that resonates with the action of the play: there are numerous moments when Willy is abandoned or suddenly realises that he is alone on stage. The phrase also epitomises the ephemeral, insubstantial and ultimately unattainable nature of The American Dream.

Use in essays on… The American Dream; Delusion.

Feminist critics often focus on Linda's role. For example, Linda Kintz (1995) observes, "her function [is] to focus the audience's gaze…on Willy … Linda, from the play's beginning, already occupies a site of loss. The domestic space of the house, ostensibly a female space, is there not in fact for her but as a space in which she must wait for Willy."

Interpretation: Feminist critics have often expressed frustration with the depiction of women in the play. Reduced to roles which are either domestic caregivers (Linda) or anonymous sex objects (The Woman), they are not portrayed in a favourable light by Miller.

Analysis:
- Kintz argues we observe Willy through Linda's eyes. With the first word of the play ("Willy!"), our first impression is of a woman waiting at home for her husband to return. "Trepidation" in her voice immediately conjures an air of concern about his arrival.
- Kintz's analysis of the domestic space onstage is a compelling one, especially considering the specificity of Miller's instructions for the set design at the opening of the play: for this playwright, the use of space is clearly evocative and symbolic.
- The "site of loss" Kintz identifies at the play's beginning is, of course, reflected in the play's ending: in both moments Willy is absent. Roudane (1997) echoed Kintz's line of analysis to argue that the play "presents a grammar of space that marginalizes Linda Loman and, by extension, all women who seem Othered, banished to the periphery of a patriarchal world."

Use in essays on… Relationships; Family; Identity.

A prolific commentator on the play, Matthew C. Roudane (1997), comments, "In Marxist terms, Willy…[reduces] himself to a commodity, an object, a thing, which enables him to make the greatest and last sale of his entire professional life: the sale of his very existence for the insurance payment."

Interpretation: Marxist interpretations of texts generally focus on representations of class, power, and wealth. The prominent thematic concern with the flaws of American capitalism render a Marxist reading of the text particularly fruitful.

Analysis:
- Roudane's argument that Willy reduces himself to a mere "commodity" to be traded for a profit paints a bleak view of the power of capitalism to overpower the individual, with the cost of Willy's life blinding him to the value of living it.
- In Miller's Requiem there is no mention of the life insurance payment: the riches that Willy dreams of leaving for his family make no difference to his modestly attended funeral. At the fall of the final curtain the ultimate sacrifice he has made for his family, his "greatest and last sale", goes unrewarded.
- Roudane stresses the overwhelming nature of capitalism on Willy – "his very existence" is consumed by pursuit of a "sale", "professional life" and "the insurance payment." However, Roudane claims Willy does this to "himself" – can one blame the individual against the forces of capitalism?

Use in essays on… The American Dream; Delusion; Identity; Legacy.

Peter Hays (2008) cites Daniel Schneider's (1950) work on Miller, highlighting how: "Willy's '*past, as in hallucination, comes back to him; not chronologically as in a flashback, but dynamically with the inner logic of his erupting volcanic unconscious. In psychiatry we call this "the return of the repressed"*'. For Schneider, the play was a version of the Oedipus myth, Biff and Happy seeking to displace Willy."

Interpretation: Psychoanalytic critics have found much to discuss in Miller's play; the original title, '*The Inside of His Head*', combined with the very deliberate choice for the set to symbolise the psyche, lends itself well to this kind of reading.

Analysis:

- Hays explores the Freudian resonances found by Schneider within the play; specifically, the Oedipal element. The Oedipus myth is the story of Oedipus, King of Thebes, who killed his father and married his mother. Psychoanalyst Sigmund Freud theorised this was a latent desire of every young man, an idea Schneider finds reflected in Biff and Happy.
- The notion of a repressed past is also significant here and students of the play may ask themselves why Willy's various flashbacks may have been repressed from his memory.
- Modern critics and students perhaps find these kind of interpretations far-fetched; it is now considered flawed to discuss, even diagnose, fictional characters as if they are real people.

Use in essays on… Relationships; Masculinity.

Performance History

In Elia Kazan's 1949 Broadway production, set designer Jo Mielziner worked closely with the director and Miller himself to realise the artistic vision, using the set to represent "the inside of his head". The family home was conjured by a skeletal structure only suggesting the boundaries between rooms, with no front façade, therefore allowing the audience an unencumbered view into the interior. The structure gave an impression of fragility which complemented the characters and themes effectively. Fluidity between spaces allowed the action of the play to take place both in Willy's home and in his mind, and in both the present and the past. Lighting and sound have also been important to the play throughout its production history to date, symbolising key themes and drawing attention to key moments.

The central role of Willy was first played by Lee J. Cobb who was only 37 years old when playing the 63-year-old Willy. More recent notable productions have featured Dustin Hoffman (1984), Brian Dennehy (1999), Philip Seymour Hoffman (2012) and Antony Sher (2015) in the lead role. Despite the apparent intention for Willy to be a man of small stature, Dennehy's performance drew acclaim for the remarkable vulnerability he was able to portray despite his imposing physique, taking to the stage as Willy Loman over 600 times. The significant decision in a 2019 London production to cast the Loman family as African American invited important racial discussions around Miller's text.

Miller himself has directed productions of the play: in Philadelphia in 1974, in Beijing in 1983, and in Stockholm in 1992. Of these, the Chinese production is perhaps the most notable given that – at that time – China had only recently emerged from the trauma of the Cultural Revolution, and that salesmen were not something audiences were familiar with. Nevertheless, the production was a great success and the play's universal themes of family relationships spoke powerfully to the Chinese audience.

How to revise effectively.

One mistake people often make is to try to revise EVERYTHING!

This is clearly not possible.

Instead, once you understand the text in detail, a good idea is to pick five or six major themes, and four or five major characters, and revise these in great detail. The same is true when exploring key scenes – you are unlikely to be able to closely analyse every single line, so focus on the *skills* of analysis and interpretation and then be ready for any question, rather than covering the whole text and trying to pre-prepare everything.

If, for example, you revised Delusion and Betrayal, you will also have covered a huge amount of material to use in questions about Masculinity, Relationships and Hope.

It is also sensible to avoid revising quotations in isolation; instead, bring together two or three textual quotations as well as a critical and contextual quotation so that any argument you make is supported and explored in detail.

Finally, make sure material is pertinent to the questions you will be set. By revising the skills of interpretation and analysis you will be able to answer the actual question set in the exam, rather than the one you wanted to come up.

Suggested Revision Activities

A great cover and repeat exercise – Cover the whole page, apart from the quotation at the top. Can you now fill in the four sections without looking – Interpretations, Techniques, Analysis, Use in essays on…?

This also works really well as **a revision activity with a friend** – cover the whole page, apart from the quotation at the top. If you read out the quotation, can they tell you the four sections without looking – Interpretations, Techniques, Analysis, Use in essays on…?

For both activities, could you extend the analysis and interpretation further, or provide an alternative interpretation? Also, can you find another quotation that extends or counters the point you have just made?

Your very own Quotation Bank! Using the same headings and format as The Quotation Bank, find 10 more quotations from throughout the text (select them from many different sections of the text to help develop whole text knowledge) and create your own revision cards.

Essay writing – They aren't always fun, but writing essays is great revision. Devise a practice question and try taking three quotations and writing out a perfect paragraph, making sure you add connectives, technical vocabulary and sophisticated language.

Glossary

Dramatic Irony – When the audience knows something the characters don't: earlier we observe a flashback to Willy's relationship with The Woman; aware of his past infidelities, we pity Linda's total devotion to a deeply flawed husband.

Flashback – A scene in which the audience are taken out of the present action and observe a scene from the past: the first of many flashbacks to moments in the family's past, the image of closeness between Willy and Biff contrasts their unsettled relationship in the present.

Foreshadowing – When the writer alludes to or makes reference to something that is yet to come in the text: the audience gets an early impression Willy may spend nights away from the family home, hinting at an untrustworthy character and foreshadowing later revelations about his infidelities.

Imagery – Figurative language that appeals to the senses of the audience: the metaphor of fire combined with the hellish – perhaps apocalyptic – imagery may foreshadow the downfall of the play's hero.

Irony – A statement that suggests one thing but often has a contrary meaning: the grim irony of Willy's death coinciding with the last mortgage payment is mirrored by the irony of Linda's repeated utterance, "We're free."

Juxtaposition – Two ideas, images or words placed next to each other to create a contrasting effect: Ben is a father figure to Willy and his exotic travels and financial success juxtapose Willy's mundane and modest lifestyle.

Language – The vocabulary chosen to create effect.

Metaphor – A word or phrase used to describe something else so that the first idea takes on the associations of the second: the pastoral metaphor "the woods are burning" is unusual for Willy, a man closely linked with the city.

Repetition – When a word, phrase or idea is repeated to reinforce it: hurried repetition of questions conveys a sense of panic from Linda – she clearly worries about Willy.

Staging – Directions given to the director or actor to aid interpretation: the densely populated urban setting, "surrounding it on all sides", invites the audience to see the struggles of the Loman family as just one example of the many families living in similar conditions with the same challenges and frustrations.

Sentence Structure – The way the writer has ordered the words in a sentence to create a certain effect: the short sentence structures and repetitive phrasing hint at Willy's disorientation and confusion, having just been distracted by a distressing memory, and realising he has been abandoned by his sons.

Symbolism – The use of a symbol to represent an idea: the symbol of the hammock is a potent one, representing the future comfort Willy aspires to achieve.

Tone – The mood or atmosphere created by the writer: the increasingly forceful tone in which Biff has to challenge Willy's delusional untruths show the audience Biff's exasperation with his father. While Biff's words intensify, Willy's assertions weaken, descending from "you were" to "you were practically".

Tri-colon – A list of three words or phrases for effect: the contrast between Willy and Singleman is stark; in the twilight of his career Willy enjoys none of the popularity ("remembered and loved and helped") he aimed to achieve.

Acknowledgements:

E Kazan: *Kazan on Directing*, published by Vintage Books 2010

A Miller: *Tragedy and the Common Man*, published by *New York Times* 1949

B Atkinson: *Death of A Salesman: Arthur Miller's Tragedy of an Ordinary Man*, published by *New York Times* 1949

C W E Bigsby: *A Critical Introduction to Twentieth-Century American Drama: Volume 2, Williams, Miller, Albee*, published by Cambridge University Press 1984

A Miller: *Timebends: A Life*, published by Methuen 1987

D Mamet: *Why Schindler is Emotional Pornography*, published by *The Guardian* 1994

A Miller: *Kaleidoscope: Miller's Tales*, on BBC Radio 4 1995

L Kintz: *The Sociosymbolic Work of Family in 'Death of A Salesman'*, from *Approaches to Teaching Miller's Death of a Salesman*, edited by M Roudane, published by The Modern Language Association of America 1995

M Roudane: *Death of A Salesman and the Poetics of Arthur Miller*, from *The Cambridge Companion to Arthur Miller*, edited by C Bigsby, published by Cambridge University Press 1997

P Hays: *Arthur Miller's Death of a Salesman*, published by Bloomsbury Academic 2008

D Schneider: *The Psychoanalyst and the Artist*, published by Farrar, Straus and Co 1950